D0429711

Walla Wa...
County Libraries

STAR WARS™

PRINCESS LEIA™

ROYAL REBEL

By Calliope Glass

Illustrated by Joe Quinones

SCHOLASTIC INC.

ISBN 978-1-338-02980-2

10 9 8 7 6 5 4 3 2 1 16 17 18 19 20

Printed in the U.S.A. 40
First printing 2016

Book design by Rick DeMonico

CONTENTS

Introduction

by General Leia Organa

To be honest, I think this whole biography thing is a bit silly. But this archival droid won't stop following me around, pestering me for details about my life. For the record, I'd much rather be *doing* things than talking about things I've already done, but maybe the droid's right—maybe my story will be useful to someone out there. At least I know it'll be entertaining—with lots of fights and plots and explosions . . . and some heartbreak, too.

In a galaxy full of marvels, I have seen things that would amaze even a thousand-year-old hyperspace pilgrim. I've learned that sometimes the most harmless-looking creatures can be the most dangerous. In fact, more than once, I have been that harmless-looking creature. At times, my appearance caused people to underestimate me. I learned to use that to my advantage. It took me a long time to discover that looking harmless can be a strength.

When I was younger—much younger—all I wanted was to show the world how strong I was. I wanted everyone to know that I wasn't simply a spoiled princess in a ruffled party dress. I wanted to prove that I could plot and fight and lead as well as any battle-hardened warrior. And prove it I did—first as a senator, then as a spy for the Rebel Alliance, and finally as a general.

Although I was raised as a princess, every new fight requires me to take on a new role. I have been at war nearly my whole life, and I have lost as many battles as I have won. But I keep fighting.

Because that's what I really am at the end of the day: a fighter.

Friends, Family, and Foes

Padmé Amidala

Leia's mother. This idealistic young politician fell in love with Jedi apprentice Anakin Skywalker, and the two were secretly married. Amidala gave birth to twins Luke and Leia but died shortly afterward.

Bail Organa

Leia's adoptive father, Bail Organa was a member of the Galactic Senate and helped form the Rebel Alliance in secret. He encouraged Leia to fight for the Rebellion.

Queen Breha Organa

Leia's adoptive mother, Breha Organa was the wise and calm queen of Alderaan. She and her husband, Bail, raised Princess Leia together. Breha and Bail both perished in the destruction of Alderaan.

R2-D2 and C-3PO

These two droids are practically family! C-3PO was originally built by Leia's biological father. R2-D2 worked for Padmé Amidala, then Anakin Skywalker, long before Leia was born. Both droids have shown tremendous loyalty and bravery when serving Leia.

Darth Vader

Raised as a slave on Tatooine, Anakin Skywalker became a Jedi apprentice to Obi-Wan Kenobi before turning to the dark side of the Force and becoming a Sith Lord with the new name of Darth Vader. Anakin was the secret husband of Amidala and the biological father of Princess Leia and Luke Skywalker.

Obi-Wan Kenobi

Obi-Wan Kenobi became a Jedi Master before disappearing into exile on Tatooine. He came to Princess Leia's aid in the fight against the Empire, only to be killed by his former apprentice Darth Vader.

Yoda

The mysterious Jedi Master who trained Luke Skywalker on Dagobah, Yoda was around 900 years old when he died, shortly before Leia helped lead the Rebel Alliance to victory over the Empire.

Luke Skywalker

Luke is Leia's twin brother, though neither of them knew about the other when they were children. Luke was raised by his aunt and uncle on Tatooine. After Obi-Wan convinced him to travel to Alderaan, Luke joined the Rebel Alliance and became Yoda's final Jedi apprentice.

Chewbacca

A Wookiee warrior and pilot, Chewbacca flew at the side of Han Solo for many years, at first as a smuggler but then as a warrior in the battle against the Empire.

Jabba the Hutt

A crime lord based on Tatooine, Jabba's last act and worst mistake was to imprison Princess Leia, who choked him to death with her chains.

Lando Calrissian

This old friend of Han Solo's was the original owner of the *Millennium Falcon*, before he became the administrator of Cloud City. He met Leia there, and eventually joined the Rebel Alliance.

Han Solo

When he met Leia, Han was a smuggler on the run from his former boss, Jabba the Hutt. But he later became a leader in the Rebel Alliance. Han and Leia married after the fall of the Empire, and had a son.

Chronology

Anakin Skywalker and Padmé Amidala meet, fall in love, and marry.

Anakin turns to the dark side and becomes Darth Vader.

Luke and Leia are born, and their mother, Padmé, dies.

While carrying plans for the Death Star to the Rebellion, Leia is captured by Vader.

As a prisoner, she witnesses the destruction of Alderaan and the death of her adopted family.

Aboard the Death Star, Leia is rescued by Han and Luke. Together they help the Rebellion destroy the Death Star.

Leia escapes from Cloud City with Lando Calrissian and helps the Rebel Alliance secretly assemble a fleet of warships.

She is captured by Jabba the Hutt while trying to rescue Han, and kills Jabba.

Leia, Han, and Luke escape Tatooine and go to the forest moon of Endor to help destroy the second Death Star.

Ben is sent to Luke for Jedi training but falls to the dark side.

Luke disappears, and in his absence the First Order rises, opposing the New Republic.

Leia sends Han to find their son, now calling himself Kylo Ren.

To hide them from their father, Obi-Wan sends Luke to Tatooine and gives Leia to the Organa family to raise as their daughter on Alderaan.

Leia grows up as a princess, and becomes a senator.

Under her father's guidance, she begins to spy for the Rebellion.

Leia helps gather together the surviving children of her home planet, Alderaan, before rejoining the Rebellion on Hoth.

The rebels' base on Hoth is discovered by the Empire. Leia flees the snowy planet with Han Solo; the two fall in love.

Leia and Han are captured by Darth Vader; Han is frozen in carbonite and given to Jabba the Hutt.

On Endor, Leia discovers that Luke is her long-lost brother, and that Darth Vader is their father.

The Rebel Alliance destroys the second Death Star and topples the Empire. Darth Vader dies.

Han and Leia help restore the Republic, marry, and have a child—Ben Solo.

Kylo Ren kills Han when Han tries to turn him back to the light.

As general, Leia leads a resistance movement against the First Order and triumphs, destroying Starkiller Base.

She sends a young Force-sensitive scavenger named Rey to bring back her brother, Luke.

CHAPTER ONE

ORIGINS

Leia was a princess of Alderaan, a planet known for its beautiful gardens and graceful architecture. In a time of galactic conflict, Alderaan set an example of peace. And on the throne of this prosperous, lovely planet sat the wise Queen Breha Organa, Leia's mother.

Her *adopted* mother, that is. Queen Breha and her husband, Senator Bail Organa, had always wanted a child of their own. They had been overjoyed to take in this tiny baby when her mother died. Leia grew up deeply loved by both of her adoptive parents.

Leia had lost her birth parents too young to remember

them, yet she did have a vague lingering memory of her mother's warmth—and her deep sadness. But because Leia had such a happy family on Alderaan, she had a happy childhood. After all, her adoptive mother was very wise and her father was very brave. What more could a little girl want?

But although her childhood was a happy one, Leia's life did not begin under happy circumstances. Leia's story actually begins many years before she was born, with the election of a new queen on a planet called Naboo. The queen was young Padmé Amidala, and she was very young indeed—just fourteen years old.

Padmé was elected queen in a landslide. She became the youngest queen to serve Naboo in many decades. With a background in political science and top marks in her classwork at the university, she confidently took on the many pressures of royal life despite her young age.

Soon, it was time for elections again on Naboo. The planet's new queen asked Padmé to continue to serve Naboo—now as a senator. On this larger, intergalactic

PROFILE

PADMÉ AMIDALA

Padmé Amidala was elected queen at the young age of fourteen for a very good reason: She was brilliant. This strong-willed young woman defended her people—and her ideals—as fiercely as an Ewok warrior defending her tree. As a senator, she served two terms; she could have had the constitution amended to allow her to stay on for another term, but she chose not to. Her grit and bravery can be seen in both her children. Although she would never know them, headstrong Luke and fearless, ambitious Leia both take after their mother.

stage, Senator Amidala worked hard to defend her ideals in the Galactic Senate. As a loyalist, her strong opinions weren't popular within the corrupt and lazy Senate. She took a firm stance against the Military Creation Act, and soon Padmé's idealism put her life in danger. She was nearly killed in an assassination attempt, and the Jedi Order sent two Jedi to serve as her bodyguards.

One of the Jedi was a knight named Obi-Wan Kenobi. The other was named Anakin Skywalker. Padmé had met them both earlier in her life, but Anakin had been just a boy. Now he was a Jedi in training. He had grown into a tall, handsome young man.

Padmé was committed to her work as a senator and claimed not to be interested in romance, but she and Anakin soon found they were falling in love.

The romance between Amidala and Anakin had to remain a secret, however. The Jedi Order did not allow its members to marry, but Anakin and Amidala wanted to make that commitment to each other. So they kept their love a secret, and they arranged a small wedding with only R2-D2 and C-3PO as guests.

Wedded bliss did not last for Amidala and Anakin. Anakin's role in the Clone Wars took him all over the galaxy, yet he still struggled to gain the trust and respect of many Jedi. Eventually he fell to the dark side of the Force, seduced by the devious Chancellor Palpatine, who was a Sith Lord named Darth Sidious. Sidious took Anakin as his Sith apprentice and renamed him Darth Vader. To gain power with the dark side, Vader stormed the Jedi Temple, leaving almost no survivors.

Horrified by the rumors, Amidala rushed to find her husband, not wanting to believe what she had heard was true. She was pregnant at the time, and died shortly after

From: Senator Bail Organa

To: Queen Breha Organa

Via: Secure Transmission

My darling, forgive my rush in writing this. I will fill in all the details as soon as I see you, which I believe will be soon indeed. This ship is scheduled to enter hyperspace in less than an hour. But I felt some warning was due to you before I appear. You will understand why when I arrive.

Terrible events - catastrophic events - have been unfolding across the galaxy. But it is heartbreaking on a more personal level. I can hardly bear to tell you, but Senator Amidala is gone - a tragedy too grim to believe.

There is more, Breha. And it will change our lives forever in a profound way. You will understand as soon as we arrive home on Alderaan.

Your loving husband,

Bail

FROM THE ARCHIVES OF THE ALDERAAN MEMORIAL ON CORUSCANT, QUEEN BREHA ORGANA COLLECTION

giving birth to twins. Vader was told that his child had died along with his wife; he did not know she had had twins. Secretly, Jedi Knight Obi-Wan Kenobi and Senator Bail Organa hid the babies far away from their evil father. Obi-Wan took Luke to a remote desert planet called Tatooine, and Organa and his wife, who was Queen of Alderaan, took in Leia.

CHAPTER TWO

THE YOUNG PRINCESS

Growing up as princess of Alderaan would have been a dream come true for many young girls across the galaxy. Everywhere, gorgeous gardens grew. Poets composed lyrical odes to everything from the small blue starflowers that bloomed in the palace lawns to the majestic mountains that towered in the distance. Music filtered through the air at almost all hours, and scholars from the farthest reaches of the galaxy arrived daily to consult Alderaan's famous libraries.

But for Leia, who loved fighting and scheming better than reciting poetry and learning about royal manners, being a princess could be a chore. Although her parents sympathized with Leia's restlessness, they were determined to make a proper princess out of her. From a young age, Leia's aunts schooled her in diplomacy—the skill of handling delicate relationships. Leia had to study galactic politics, manners, and rhetoric, which is the art of effective speaking.

Even though she was intelligent and clever, these lessons were difficult for Leia. She felt useless and trapped when she was sitting in a classroom. She yawned and fidgeted her way through composition classes and diplomacy workshops. Sometimes, when she was stuck in the same place too long, she'd start to mumble to herself. Under her breath, she'd call her inane lessons—and sometimes her tedious tutors—creative and disparaging names. She didn't mean to hurt anyone's feelings, but she *had* to vent somehow. Of course, she never got caught; she was always quick with an inspired explanation.

What Leia longed to do was to take action. She

didn't see the point in learning the names of every single queen of Alderaan who had come before her mother. She wanted to make a name for *herself*, instead.

Leia's parents finally decided to let her learn some good old-fashioned fighting in addition to the nuances of interplanetary politics.

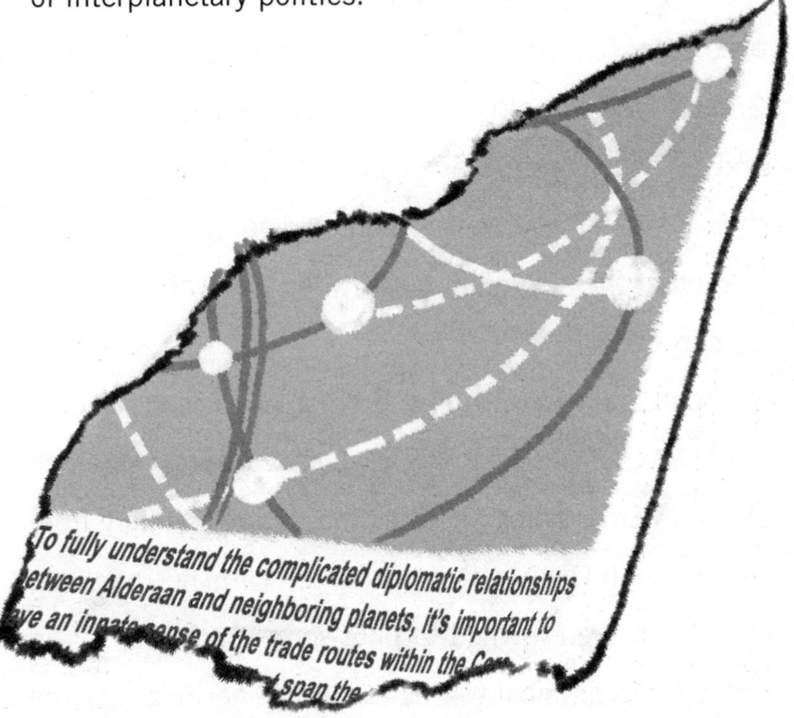

A PRINCESS OF ALDERAAN IS EXPECTED TO KNOW ENDLESS DETAILS ABOUT GALACTIC POLITICS. MANY OF LEIA'S DAYS WERE SPENT STUDYING TEXTS LIKE THIS ONE.

"We might as well," they finally told each other. After all, both of Leia's parents knew that being a princess was often a dangerous business. Given her parents' wealth and importance, Leia was in constant danger of being abducted. And beyond that, the galaxy was in a period of great change. If the political tensions increased, not even royal families or galactic senators would be safe. Breha and Bail both knew a great deal about fighting, and both had permanent guards. Although they loved their daughter and worked hard to keep her safe, they knew that the day might come when she would need to defend herself.

Soon, along with her diplomacy and dancing lessons, Leia was learning to shoot a blaster, to knock down a warrior twice her size, and to ride anything from a speeder bike to a flying thranta. With her mother's help, Leia even learned to pilot some small ships. The demanding physical workouts cleared her head for the mind-numbing boredom of her more traditional lessons.

Leia was much happier now.

QUEEN BREHA ORGANA

As queen and minister of education for Alderaan, Breha was a very important person on a very important planet. She was loved as a ruler and deeply respected by her peers. She was committed to her family as well.

In addition to these responsibilities, Queen Breha considered it her duty to mentor a select group of pupils in combat and the heritage of Alderaan. After all, she wasn't just the queen—she was also a master of several forms of hand-to-hand fighting. (Not many people—not even her daughter—knew this about her.)

Leia's father encouraged her fiery spirit and her keen sense of justice. During Leia's childhood, Bail Organa was both serving on the Imperial Senate and also quietly helping form the Rebel Alliance. As an idealist, he was determined to defeat the Empire and restore the Galactic Republic. And he hoped his young daughter would follow in his footsteps.

Leia's father was a role model for her rebellious nature, but her mother was a cooler, steadier influence.

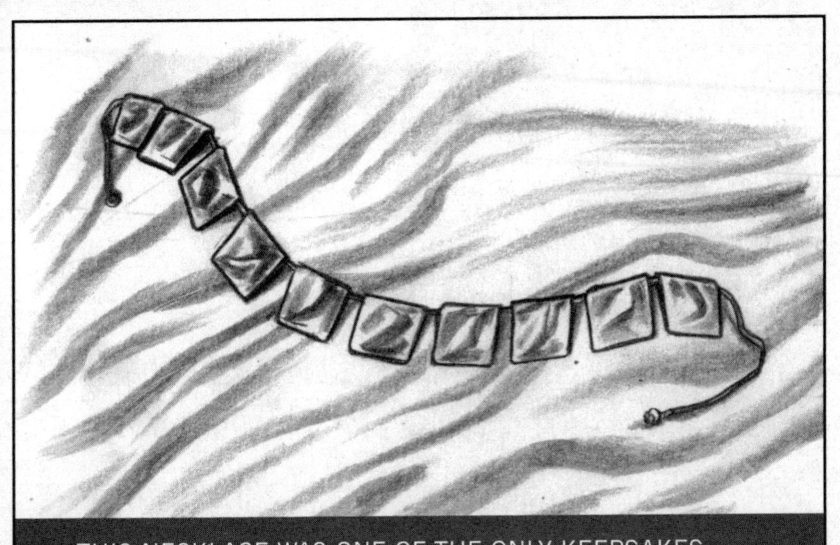

THIS NECKLACE WAS ONE OF THE ONLY KEEPSAKES LEIA HAD OF HER ADOPTIVE MOTHER. SHE WORE IT FOR FORMAL CEREMONIES, SUCH AS THE MEDAL CEREMONY ON YAVIN 4 FOLLOWING THE ALLIANCE'S SUCCESSFUL ATTACK AGAINST THE FIRST DEATH STAR.

Queen Breha was very smart, and understood the value of diplomacy. She ruled Alderaan with a kind and even hand. The citizens of the planet loved her for her fairness, but Breha wasn't always quiet and gentle. When there was a crisis, she was quick to respond. She was the perfect queen for one of the most important planets in the galaxy.

CHAPTER THREE

AN ALLIANCE SPY

The years flew by. Soon, Leia was a teenager, and she had learned a lot about being a princess—and a rebel—from both her mother and father. She had also learned a great deal about diplomacy and galactic politics . . . and had finally started taking some real interest in those topics. In her studies, Leia had learned enough to realize that something was deeply wrong with the Galactic Empire.

The Empire was abusive to its people. While things appeared uneventful in the Core Worlds like Alderaan, the Outer Rim was quite another matter. Out there,

PROFILE

BAIL ORGANA

Bail Organa understood the power of the dark side all too well. He had seen the great Jedi Anakin consumed by it. Although Bail and Anakin had fought together in the Clone Wars, any connection they had died the day that Anakin became Darth Vader and the Empire took over the Republic. Bail vowed to fight the new Empire and to restore the Republic. With help from his adopted daughter Princess Leia and many others who shared the same goal, he set the Rebel Alliance on the track to defeating the Empire for good. He never told Leia the identity of her birth father.

the Empire didn't hesitate to send ordinary citizens to internment camps, or to execute anyone suspected of opposing the Empire. Word of these atrocities reached Leia through her parents and their friends.

There was something rotten at the core of the Galactic Empire, and Leia was determined to help set things right. She didn't want to continue with her classwork, day to day, pretending the galaxy was not in peril. When she couldn't take it anymore, she went to her father, listing all of her concerns and grievances with the Empire.

Bail Organa had been waiting for this day for a long time. As soon as Leia came to him with her fears and frustrations, he quietly invited her into a secret organization. It was a group he helped found called the Alliance to Restore the Republic. Even though he was a senator and was active in the government of the galaxy, Bail Organa had been as frustrated as Leia. In hopes of making a difference and taking a stand against the Empire, he had started a rebellion. Its aim was to strike back directly at the Emperor and all those who supported his corrupt regime. Under the leadership of Bail Organa, Mon Mothma, and other prominent individuals, the Rebel Alliance was quickly growing in size and power. People from all over the galaxy were banding together to fight back against the oppressive Empire.

"Politics didn't work," Bail told his daughter, "so now it's war."

Leia signed on at once. She was excited about being a part of the Rebel Alliance. At last, she would get a chance to do something worth doing! At last, she would be able to make a difference. As a daughter of a senator and a proper princess—Leia could accept missions that had the appearance of peacekeeping efforts or acts of good will.

One of her early missions was to deliver ships to rebels on the distant planet of Lothal. It would not be easy to pull off. Bail Organa knew that he was being watched closely. The Empire suspected that Alderaan had provided ships to the rebel cause in the past, but they lacked proof. If the Empire gained evidence that the "peaceful planet" was assisting the rebel cause, Alderaan would lose its seats in the Imperial Senate,

and Leia's father would be arrested as a traitor.

Leia presented an intricate plan to Bail and other Alliance leaders. *She* would travel to Lothal, carrying rescue supplies for the occupied planet on three large ships. While she was there, she'd allow the rebels to "steal" her ships. In this scheme, the rebels would get the ships they needed, but Alderaan would not be caught for supplying them. The Empire could not blame Leia if the ships were stolen.

It was a clever scheme, and Leia was proud of it. That much was clear when she arrived on Lothal and began giving the local rebels, Ezra Bridger and Kanan Jarrus, direct orders. But not all went as planned. The Empire was prepared. One of its lieutenants actually told Leia that he knew Alderaan had a "habit" of losing its ships and he put the three cruisers she brought to Lothal under gravity locks. Leia and the rebels would need to come up with a new plan. Leia quickly gained respect for just how spontaneous and innovative the rebels had to be in order to salvage a mission.

Leia earned a fair amount of respect as well. Rebel Ezra Bridger even asked her why she, a princess, chose to join the battle. "I feel that because I can fight, I have to. For those who cannot," Leia replied.

While Leia got a thrill from being involved in proper spy work, it didn't come often. And no matter what the Rebel Alliance tried, it was clear that the Empire was only growing stronger.

As soon as she was old enough, Leia ran for a seat on the Imperial Senate. She was going to make a difference for her people. As a part of the government, she would force the Empire to reform—from within. One of the youngest senators ever, Leia stood fast against the wickedness of the Empire in the Senate. Every day at the Senate, she spoke out about the injustices being committed by Imperial forces throughout the galaxy. But nobody took her seriously. Nobody else in the Senate wanted to defend the people—they just

LEIA'S OFFICIAL SENATE BADGE.

wanted to defend their own selfish interests. Or to stay safe. Either her fellow politicians were too corrupt or too frightened to join her in her attempts at reform. With her outspoken protests, Leia was making herself very unpopular with the Empire leadership.

But her position as a senator could also serve as a guise. She could claim that she was traveling the galaxy on business of the Imperial Senate.

Guided by her father—and by her innate sense of justice—Leia divided her time between her secret life as a spy and her public life as a politician. She kept up appearances as a senator, quietly attending the Senate as before. But at the same time, Leia was eager to do whatever she could for the Rebel Alliance.

Soon, Leia was handed her most important mission. The Empire was making a huge weapon—nobody knew much about it, because it was top secret. But some rebel fighters had gotten their hands on the plans for this weapon. Leia's job was to deliver the plans to the Rebellion leaders, and she needed to recruit one of her

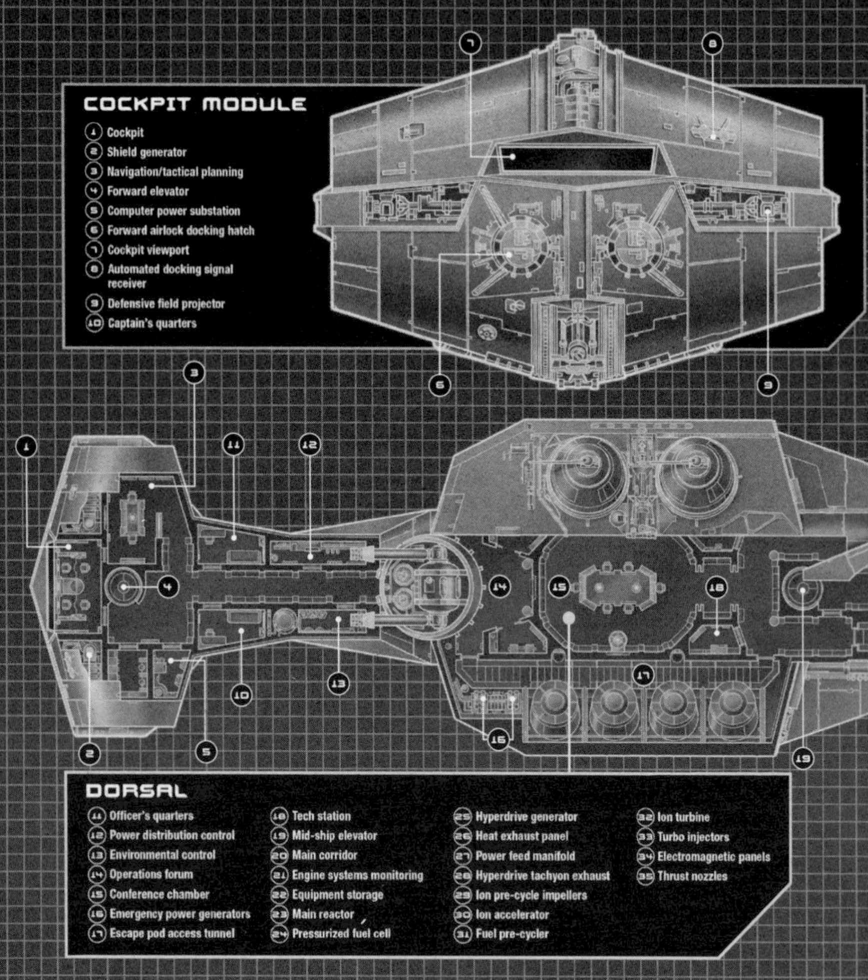

father's old allies in the process.

But disaster struck: Leia's ship, the *Tantive IV*, was intercepted by the Empire. As Imperial troops began to blast their way on board, Leia thought fast. With the Empire taking control of her ship, she knew she had to

A BLUEPRINT OF LEIA'S SHIP, THE *TANTIVE IV*. THIS MODEL IS THE CORELLIAN CORVETTE, AND IT HAD MANY USES: CARGO, TROOP TRANSPORT, AND PASSENGER CARRIER. THE REBEL FLEET EVENTUALLY INCLUDED SEVERAL OF CORELLIAN CORVETTES. THE MODEL EARNED THE NICKNAME "BLOCKADE RUNNER," AS THE ALLIANCE OFTEN USED IT TO ESCAPE IMPERIAL TRAPS.

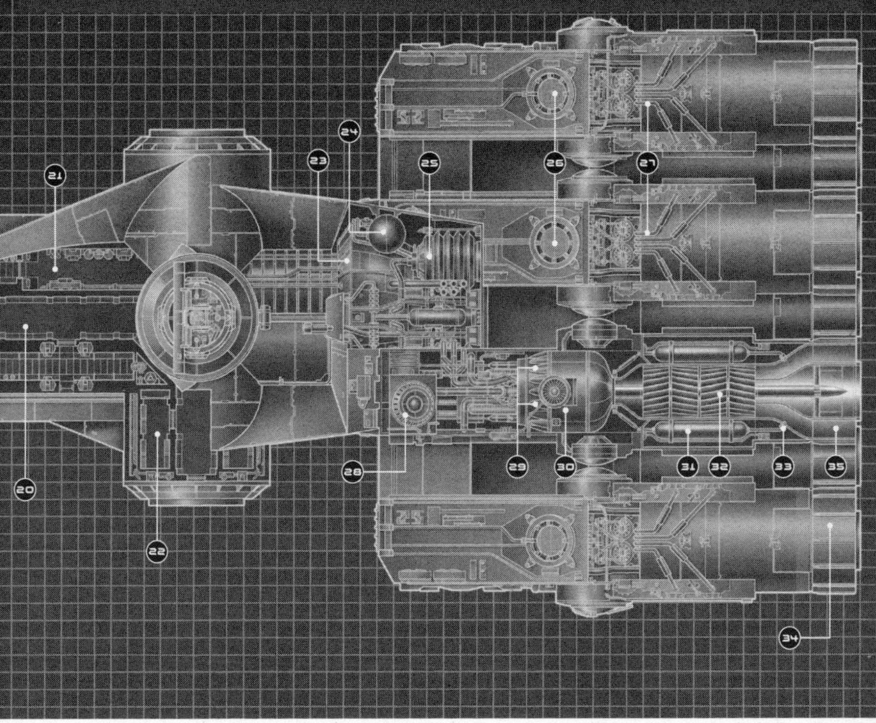

get those plans off the ship and into safe hands. And it was clear that she could not do so herself.

Thinking quickly, Leia considered her ship's location. Tatooine! They were nearing Tatooine, which was the forsaken planet where her new recruit was said to live.

"Obi-Wan Kenobi," Leia murmured to herself. Her father had spoken of the old Jedi Master often, as they had fought together in the Clone Wars. But Obi-Wan had avoided being involved in the Alliance up to this point. He had become a hermit, living alone in a remote, sandy stretch of the desert planet.

Leia knew what she had to do, and she knew who could help her do it.

Luckily, the very astromech droid she had in mind happened to roll by. The droid, named R2-D2, had proved very capable in the past.

PROFILE

R2-D2

Perhaps the most famous astromech droid ever, R2-D2 worked for Leia's mother, Padmé Amidala, long before he worked for Bail Organa, Leia, and then Luke. He even served as Anakin Skywalker's co-pilot during the Clone Wars for a time. With many hidden tools, arms, and containers, R2-D2 was always full of surprises. But the most surprising thing about him was his personality: He could be irreverent at times, and he was unusually loyal for a droid.

CHAPTER FOUR

CAPTURED BY VADER

Working quickly, Leia recorded a holomessage for General Kenobi and gave R2-D2 the plans for the Death Star. She made the droid's mission clear: to find Obi-Wan on Tatooine.

Now all that was left was for R2-D2 to get himself off the ship and to safety. Leia knew he would need some time to find an escape pod and flee the ship. It was vital that he escape before the Imperial troops discovered that he had the plans.

Leia could hear the stormtroopers approaching, so she grabbed a blaster and started making trouble.

PROFILE

C-3PO

Famously fussy, this protocol droid often got on his friend R2-D2's nerves. But his skill with languages came in handy. He was programmed in over six million kinds of communication. Originally built and wired by Anakin Skywalker with parts from Watto's junk shop, C-3PO later became a translator for diplomatic meetings and rebel missions. Underneath that scaredy-cat shell, C-3PO's heart was pure gold.

Her aim was to avoid being captured, yet this skirmish also provided extra time for the droid.

While Leia distracted the Imperial troops, R2-D2 and his friend C-3PO took full advantage of the chaos and piled into an escape pod. Soon the two droids were on their way to Tatooine—and to Obi-Wan Kenobi!

Leia gave as good as she got, but soon the Imperial troops subdued her. She was shackled and dragged through the smoking passageways of her own battered ship. Before long, she was face-to-face with none other than Darth Vader himself!

Leia knew all too well how dangerous and evil Vader was. Even as a child, Leia had known to fear the black-helmeted ghoul who did the Emperor's dirty work. But now that she was in his presence—with a Rebel Alliance mission in jeopardy—she was determined not to let Vader know how scared she was.

"Lord Vader," Leia said scornfully. "I should have known. Only you could be so bold."

Leia knew that Vader had no actual evidence that

she was anything other than a peaceful senator doing the Empire's work. So she decided to deny everything. She took a deep breath, and began to stonewall the Emperor's own right-hand man.

"I'm a member of the Imperial Senate on a diplomatic mission to Alderaan," Leia said haughtily. But Vader wasn't having it.

"You're a part of the Rebel Alliance," he snarled, "and a traitor. Take her away!"

Soon, Leia was escorted on board the mysterious weapon itself—a giant battle station called the Death Star. It was as big as a moon. She was thrown into a holding cell by two stormtroopers. She wondered how

many other unfortunate enemies of the Empire were being held on the strange battle station, and if anyone had ever escaped.

Soon her interrogation at the hands of Darth Vader began. It was awful, but Leia was comforted to know that R2-D2 must have escaped. They wouldn't care so much about what she knew if they'd captured the little droid—and the plans he carried. Now, she just hoped he would find Obi-Wan Kenobi.

Leia had been trained to resist torture—it was part of the training all royals received. But the torments Darth Vader's interrogation droid put her through were almost too much to bear. Leia was hanging on by a thread by the time she was brought before Governor Tarkin. She knew her father had no respect for Tarkin, who was another of the Emperor's thugs. Whenever she'd met the man at a diplomatic dinner, she'd had to hold her tongue. There was no need to restrain herself anymore.

"I should have expected to find you holding Vader's leash," Leia told Tarkin haughtily. "I recognized your

DARTH VADER

Born Anakin Skywalker, this Force-sensitive warrior renounced his name—and the Jedi Order—when he turned to the dark side of the Force. Vader became the Emperor's enforcer, prowling the galaxy and brutally suppressing all attempts to oppose the Empire. It wasn't until Luke and Leia were fully grown that Vader realized he was a father—and that his children were fighting on the opposite side of the war.

foul stench when I was brought on board."

On a screen, a green planet floated, calm and beautiful in the blackness of space. It was Alderaan—Leia's home planet.

Vader and Tarkin tried to get Leia to reveal the location of the current rebel base, this time by threatening her homeworld. Leia stayed silent for a long time, but the princess's love of her planet was strong—they had been smart to use Alderaan against her. Finally, Leia gave in . . . or appeared to. She named the location of an old rebel base on Dantooine. It had already been abandoned—but Vader and Tarkin didn't know that.

Tarkin nodded. "Continue with the operation," he commanded. "You may fire when ready."

It is hard to imagine how profound Leia's grief must have been as she helplessly watched her home—and all the people living on it—get blown to space dust before her very eyes.

CHAPTER FIVE

A PRINCESS AT WAR

Leia was thrown back into her cell after witnessing the destruction of Alderaan. The princess wasn't a fool—she knew that now that she'd given up that old rebel base location, the next step for her was termination. They were going to kill her.

But when a stormtrooper arrived to collect Leia from her cell, there was something off about him. For one thing, he was unusually short for a stormtrooper.

"I'm Luke Skywalker," he said. Then he pulled his helmet off, which was strictly against regulations. He definitely wasn't a stormtrooper. "I'm here to rescue you."

As soon as Luke Skywalker said that he had come with Obi-Wan Kenobi, Leia rushed out of the cell in a flash. They immediately ran into another man dressed as a stormtrooper—Han Solo—and a Wookiee named Chewbacca. They were also part of the rescue mission. Dodging blaster fire, they realized they were trapped in the cell-block corridor. Actual stormtroopers were at the other end, blocking their escape.

Leia was glad this crew had come to rescue her, but she wished they were a little better at it. For one thing, Leia found Han Solo to be incredibly annoying. Although he clearly didn't have a plan, he was still acting as though he was in charge. Princess Leia Organa was a senator and a rebel spy, and she didn't like being bossed around, especially by people who weren't as qualified as she was. Leia decided to take charge and grabbed Luke's blaster.

"Somebody has to save our skins," she said. She expertly fired a couple of shots at the closest stormtroopers, and then led Han, Chewbacca, and Luke into a garbage chute. The four tumbled into the stinking pool of garbage. They were safe from stormtroopers, but now they had a new problem: They had ended up in a giant trash compactor! As the walls closed in around them, Luke desperately radioed his droid friends for help, and Leia learned it was C-3PO and R2-D2. Just in time, R2-D2 was able to stop the compactor from crushing Leia and her rescuers to death.

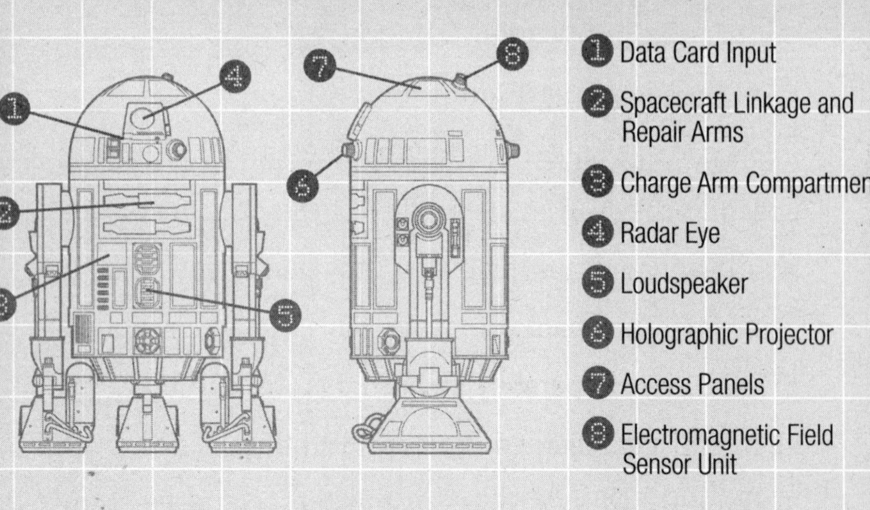

ASTROMECH DROIDS LIKE R2-D2 WERE DESIGNED TO DIAGNOSE AND FIX MECHANICAL PROBLEMS ON SHIPS, AS WELL AS CALCULATE THE JUMP TO HYPERSPACE. WITH VARIOUS TOOLS, THEY CAN TAP INTO A VARIETY OF COMPUTER SYSTEMS AND OVERRIDE COMMANDS.

Now all that was left was to sneak back into the main halls of the Death Star and make it to Solo's ship, the *Millennium Falcon*, in the hangar. As Leia ran with her rescuers toward the ship, Luke skidded to a halt. "Look!" he cried, pointing. On the other side of the hangar, Darth Vader was fighting an old, cloaked man. They were both using odd, old-fashioned weapons that looked like swords made of fiery light.

As they scrambled into their escape craft, Darth Vader struck down the old man. His robes collapsed around him as though his body had simply vaporized.

"No!" screamed Luke.

Leia and Han dragged Luke on board the ship, and soon they had made their escape from the Death Star.

Leia was saddened by the death of Obi-Wan Kenobi, the hero she had never met. But that sorrow didn't compare with Leia's concern about the Death Star. She'd seen what it could do—she'd seen it destroy her home planet in seconds—and she knew how important it was to warn the leadership of the Rebellion about it. The Empire had to be stopped.

The good news was that R2-D2 and C-3PO had made it back to the *Millennium Falcon* as well. R2-D2 still had the stolen plans, so Leia had a chance to complete her mission. Leia and her new friends sped to the rebel base on Yavin 4 and delivered the plans to the rebel leaders. Once they arrived, they learned there was not a moment to waste—the Death Star had tracked Han Solo's ship to Yavin. The giant battle station was coming, and it would soon destroy the rebel base!

Leia and her fellow rebels quickly analyzed the Death Star readouts that R2-D2 had carried safely with him. The giant battle station must have taken decades to build. The plans were almost perfect. *Almost.* There

OBI-WAN KENOBI

Obi-Wan Kenobi was a Jedi, originally an apprentice to Qui-Gon Jinn. When Jinn was killed by Darth Maul, Kenobi became a Jedi Knight and took on young Anakin Skywalker as his Padawan. After Anakin turned to the dark side and became Darth Vader, Obi-Wan helped Bail Organa hide the Dark Lord's children from him, and went into exile in the deserts of Tatooine. He emerged decades later to help Luke Skywalker rescue Leia—and died at Vader's hand.

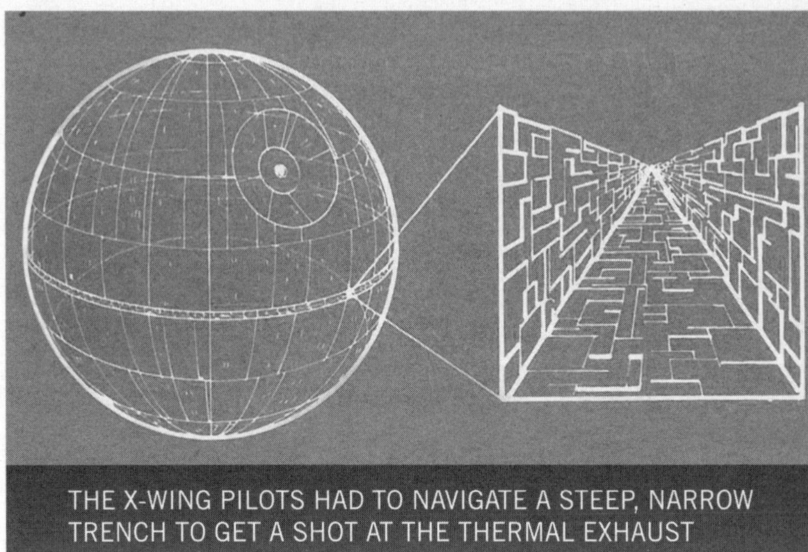

THE X-WING PILOTS HAD TO NAVIGATE A STEEP, NARROW TRENCH TO GET A SHOT AT THE THERMAL EXHAUST PORT, WHICH WOULD LEAD TO THE CORE REACTOR.

was one small flaw—and that flaw would help the rebels destroy it!

The rebels' only hope was that one of their pilots would be sharp enough to get a shot straight down the Death Star's exhaust port. It was the station's only weak point, but a direct hit would annihilate it. Fighter pilots left the rebel base immediately; Luke was among them. Leia remained at the base, overseeing the action.

Leia checked the stats of Luke's X-wing squadron again. It was good that he was flying with Red Squadron—the group was made up of great pilots. The last thing

Leia needed was to worry about her new friend's safety. Especially since she didn't really have many friends at all. On Alderaan, she'd had servants, but very few peers. All her classes were one-on-one with royal tutors. And then, as a senator and spy, most of the people Leia worked with were much older than she was. They were co-conspirators, but not really friends. Luke and Han, though—they had quickly become Leia's friends as well as her allies. So it was natural that the princess was especially concerned about Luke, who had committed himself to the Alliance with no reservations at all.

Luckily, he had good pilots watching his back in the fray.

A heated battle took place along the surface of the enormous Death Star, as X-wing fighters fended off TIE fighters, and the rebel pilots looked for a chance to hit their target.

Leia witnessed many rebel ships go down—and many rebel pilots die—before Luke Skywalker was able to go in for the crucial shot. But then a TIE fighter homed in on him, and it was Han Solo in the *Millennium Falcon* who swooped in and got the fighter off Luke's tail! Luke then managed to land a shot directly down the exhaust port of the Death Star. A chain reaction started deep in the heart of the terrible weapon, and soon it exploded violently, showering sparks through the entire star system.

The Death Star was gone. From the base, Leia watched the triumphant conclusion of the battle. When Luke's X-wing landed at the base, she ran to her new friend and tackled him with a hug. And Han got a hug, too. After all, even though he had said he was only in it for the money, he had come through in the big battle! Princess Leia suspected there was more to Han than what had appeared at first glance.

Thanks to Leia's grit as a spy and her talents as a newly formed rebel leader, the Empire had suffered a terrible blow. The rebels had scored a major victory.

Later, Princess Leia stood on a dais and faced many squadrons of gathered rebel fighters as she awarded

HAN SOLO'S MEDAL OF BRAVERY, AWARDED BY PRINCESS LEIA ORGANA.

medals to Luke Skywalker and Han Solo for their bravery.

To many of the rebels assembled at the ceremony that day, Leia appeared to be surprisingly cold and collected. They were surprised at such calm from a woman who had recently lost her parents—and her entire planet. Some of the rebel troops were even heard to criticize her, wondering why she didn't show any human emotion.

But to Princess Leia, the most important thing was the Alliance. Now, with all she had lost, it had to be. In order to be a strong rebel leader, she needed to look like a strong rebel leader . . . not a young woman who had lost nearly everything. Even if that's what she was.

Knowing everything we do about Princess Leia Organa, we can assume that her sorrow on that day was matched only by her certainty that her parents would have been pleased with the rebels' success. No doubt, they would have been proud of the princess—and the rebel—that their daughter had become.

CHAPTER SIX

ESCAPE FROM HOTH

The Rebel Alliance had struck the Empire a terrible blow. With the destruction of the Death Star, the rebels could now aim to gather their forces for a final battle. Soon, the Republic would be restored. Or so Leia hoped.

If Leia struggled with grief—if she found herself often thinking of her missing planet and her dead parents—well, that was her business, and not something she shared with others. After all, she had an Empire to defeat.

The Alliance needed Princess Leia. With Bail Organa dead, she had to step into his shoes. She had to be a leader for the rebels, and she was ready to take charge. But there was something else Leia was determined to do first.

Defying the orders of the other rebel leaders, Leia ventured out into the galaxy with an Alderaanian pilot named Evaan Verlaine. Their mission was to find as many surviving Alderaanians as they could. The Empire was hunting down anyone from Alderaan who hadn't been on the planet when it was destroyed. Leia couldn't let that happen. She was determined to save the rest of her people.

This mission was a crucial experience for Leia. She was operating independently—making her own decisions, without the help of other rebel leaders. She had to prove her worth as a spy, convincing as many people as possible to assist her in completing her plan.

It was also on this mission that Leia was forced to accept her title of "princess" in a different way. When she was a child, "princess" was a title that meant "don't run indoors, don't laugh too loudly, and always remember your manners." But now Leia's rank as princess of Alderaan meant something else entirely. It meant that she was the only known surviving member of the royal house of a dead planet. She felt the responsibility of being the one person in the galaxy who

could find, save, and unite the surviving children of the planet of Alderaan.

Although Leia and Evaan encountered many near-death dangers on their mission, they completed it. Leia was able to return to her duties as a rebel leader knowing that her obligations as the last princess of Alderaan had been fulfilled. Her people—what remained of them—were safe.

When Leia arrived on the new rebel base, she found it was very different from the one she'd known on Yavin. For security measures, the Alliance had moved their operations to Hoth, an ice planet. It was bitterly, dangerously cold all the time. The snow flew thick and blinding. And the base itself was in a cave.

But Luke was there, and so was Han. Leia held the farm boy from Tatooine in high regard. She admired his commitment to the rebel cause. But she fought constantly with the handsome, rascally Han Solo.

CARVED OUT OF A GLACIER AND LOCATED ON AN UNINHABITED PLANET IN A REMOTE SYSTEM, ECHO BASE APPEARED NEARLY UNDETECTABLE. HERE, MILITARY LEADERS OF THE REBELLION PLANNED THEIR NEXT MOVE AGAINST THE EMPIRE.

LUKE SKYWALKER

Raised by his aunt and uncle on the remote planet of Tatooine, Luke Skywalker grew up on a moisture farm. He longed to leave the dull chores of farm life and seek adventure with the rebels in the Galactic Civil War. Little did he dream that he would eventually help *win* the fight against the Empire, by defeating his own father.

Han seemed to find Leia as annoying as she found him. He told her she was bossy and high-minded and used to getting her way. And he was right. She had grown up a princess, and she was accustomed to being right. The two were at each other's throats day and night. After a while, the other rebels at the Hoth base got used to it; it wasn't uncommon to find the princess

and the smuggler fighting in a busy hallway while rebel business was carried out around them.

All too soon, the Empire tracked down the rebels on Hoth. Their secret base was a secret no more. Leia and the other rebel leaders ordered an evacuation immediately. The rebels would have to find a new base . . . again.

Leia insisted on staying on the base until the final wave of the evacuation. She briefed the pilots on their roles in battling the invading Imperial army and planned to leave only when everyone else was safely off the planet. By then, Imperial troops had already entered the base! Leia, Han, and Chewbacca escaped by the skin of their teeth. The Empire was hot on their trail as they blasted into space, so Han steered the *Millennium Falcon* into an asteroid field. Dodging between the asteroids, he outmaneuvered the Empire's ships.

As soon as there was a chance, Han skillfully piloted the *Falcon* into a cave on a large asteroid. They had escaped. Even Leia was impressed. Safe in the heart of

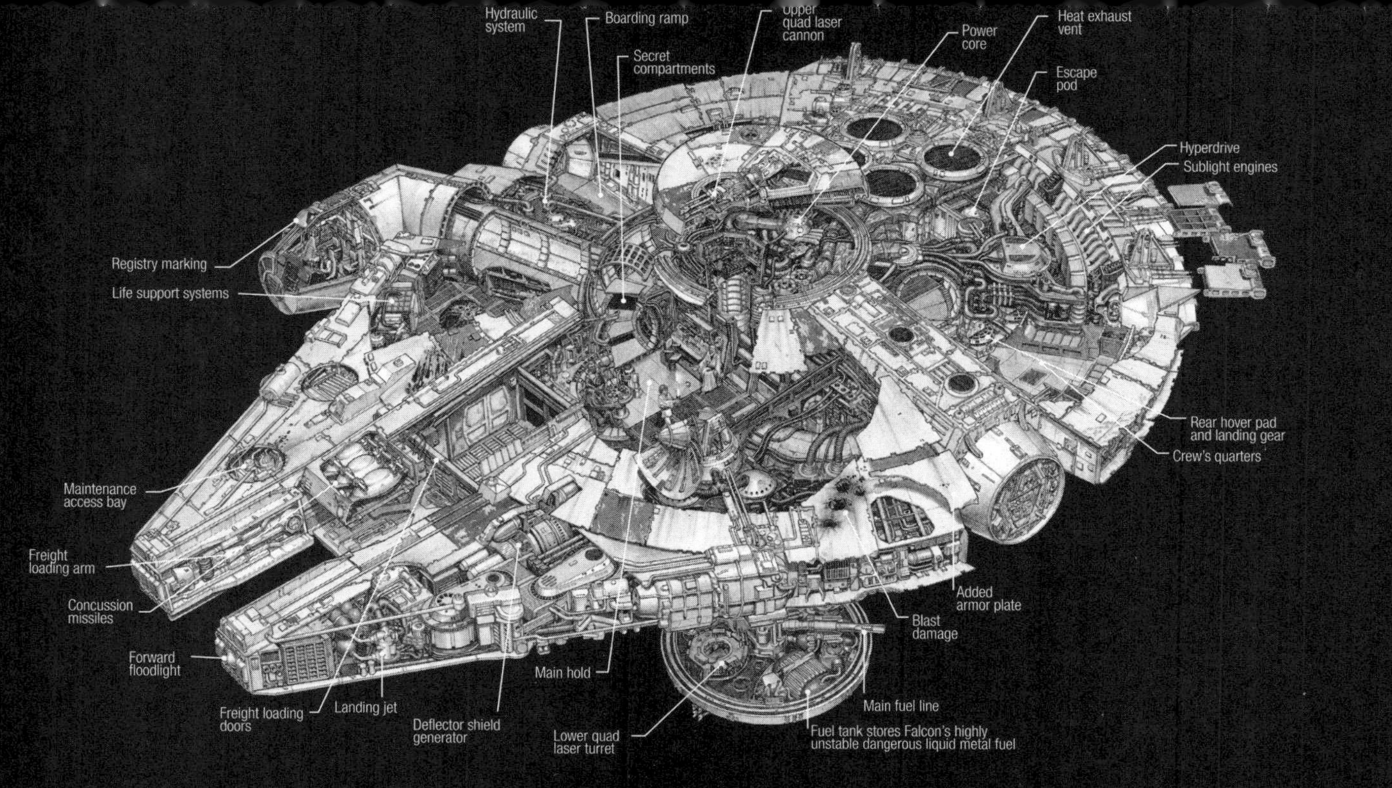

WITH MANY CUSTOM FEATURES FOR SMUGGLING, THE MILLENNIUM FALCON WAS NOT JUST ANY FREIGHTER. IT HAD TREMENDOUS SPEED, HAVING MADE THE KESSEL RUN IN LESS THAN 12 PARSECS, A RECORD.

YODA

As ancient as he was wise, this tiny green Jedi Master's origins are lost to the mists of time. Nobody even knows what species he was. He had many Jedi apprentices during his 900 years, but Luke Skywalker was his last.

the asteroid, they worked on repairs to the ship. Leia and Han also finally figured out why they had been fighting so much. It turned out the two were very much in love.

If Leia wondered what Luke would think of her new romance with Han, she certainly didn't mention it out loud. And Luke wasn't there, in any case—he had gone his own way when they fled Hoth, to train with a mysterious old Jedi Master named Yoda on the planet Dagobah.

Any sense of calm for Leia and Han ended all too soon. First, meddling space bats called mynocks attacked the *Millennium Falcon*! Then, as soon as they had driven the horrible beasts off, the cave they were in erupted into motion. It wasn't a cave after all—it was the gullet of a space slug! Han piloted the *Falcon* out of the huge creature's mouth just in time.

CHAPTER SEVEN

BETRAYAL IN CLOUD CITY

Princess Leia and Han desperately needed to rejoin the rebel fleet. But the hyperspace drive on the *Millennium Falcon* was broken, and the ship couldn't go to lightspeed. Leia was furious and frustrated. Even Han's co-pilot, the Wookiee Chewbacca, was angry. Leia suspected that Chewbacca must have the patience of a Jedi to have put up with Han—and his unreliable ship—for all those years.

Luckily, Han had a friend nearby—an old smuggling buddy named Lando Calrissian, who was now the administrator of a city above the planet Bespin. They

PROFILE

CHEWBACCA

Han Solo's Wookiee co-pilot was a crack shot, a fierce warrior, and a surprisingly tenderhearted fellow. He and Han worked together for most of Han's life, first as smuggling partners and then as heroes in the Galactic Civil War. It was Chewbacca who convinced Han not to leave after getting their reward for delivering Princess Leia.

headed for Cloud City right away, and were greeted warmly by Lando. Although Leia didn't trust him, she did appreciate how polite he was. That alone set him apart from Han Solo, who, though charming, could be very rude.

The chambers Lando gave Leia were luxurious and beautiful, and she received sophisticated and stylish new clothing. Leia would have enjoyed herself if she weren't so worried that something was going to go wrong at any minute. Her instincts were screaming warnings at her.

And, in fact, no sooner had they settled in at Cloud City than Lando betrayed them to Darth Vader!

"I had no choice," Lando said, with sincere regret. "They arrived right before you did."

Vader loomed over them, his black mask as blank and terrifying as always. Leia had hoped never to see Darth Vader again, and here he was in the same room with her and the man she loved.

It turned out the whole thing was a trap—for Luke. Vader knew that the best way to get at Luke was through his friends. He knew that Luke would sense they were in danger. Their suffering would draw Luke to Cloud City, where Vader was lying in wait for him.

Leia tried to come up with a plan—but she couldn't think of anything. Their situation was terrible. It was bad enough that they were in the hands of Vader . . . now he was going to get Luke, too. And the crime lord Jabba the Hutt was going to get Han. Leia felt helpless as she watched Han being led to the carbonite chamber. "I love you," she blurted out, wishing her confession could come any other way. Then she could only watch as Han was frozen in carbonite, and a bounty hunter took him away.

But at the last moment, Lando saved the day. Even though he had betrayed them to Vader in order to protect Cloud City, he had second thoughts and realized he couldn't let Vader get away with it. Leia, Lando, and Chewbacca fled to the *Millennium Falcon* and finally made their escape.

As they were fleeing, Leia suddenly ordered Lando to turn back. Both Lando and Chewbacca were shocked—why would they return to Cloud City when Vader was

there? But Leia knew that Luke was there, too. She didn't know how she knew it . . . she just did.

Force sensitivity runs in families. At that time, Leia had no idea that she was a Skywalker by birth, but her heritage emerged at that moment. And it's a good thing, because Luke was near death by the time the *Millennium Falcon* rescued him from the underside of Cloud City, where he was barely clinging on. If Leia hadn't been in tune with the Force (even though she had no idea of her powers), Luke never would have survived.

It's easy to imagine how worried Leia must have been. Somewhere out there, Han was being delivered to Jabba the Hutt. Vader and the Emperor were plotting the destruction of the Alliance. The Empire was continuing its reign of tyranny throughout the galaxy. And on top of it all, Leia's people were still gone, her parents still dead. Leia was strong—she would rise to the occasion. But even a strong leader has her moments of silent despair.

Luke Skywalker wasn't in much better shape than Leia. He had come away from his fight against Darth

Vader pale and quiet, and with one hand missing. He had to have surgery to get a new, mechanical hand. But something even more terrible had happened to him on Bespin, and Leia didn't know what it was. She knew better than to ask—some hurts took time to share.

In the weeks that followed, Leia threw herself into her work for the Rebel Alliance. She'd proven her worth as a rebel leader, and now she was part of the inner circle. The stakes were high, and Leia had huge responsibilities. Although she wanted to find and rescue

THE CYBERNETIC HAND LUKE SKYWALKER WAS GIVEN AFTER HIS FIGHT WITH DARTH VADER IN CLOUD CITY.

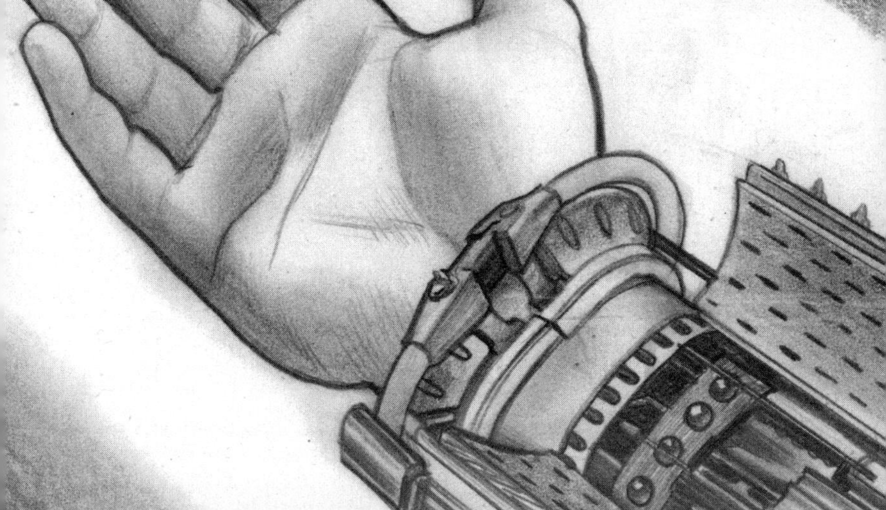

Han, her work for the Rebellion was too urgent. At this point, the rebels needed to gather a fleet of warships, but they couldn't do that with the Empire on high alert. Propelled by her duty, Leia and a crew headed to an outer system of the Empire. Her job was to lay a false trail for the Imperial military to follow. If Leia could keep the Empire busy, leading them on a merry chase through the backwaters of the galaxy, the other rebels could recruit a fleet closer to home.

If Leia's goal was to distract the Empire, she was also distracting herself; with her mind firmly on her work for the Rebellion, she didn't have much time to worry about Han. His situation was very worrisome indeed.

CHAPTER EIGHT

THE DEATH OF JABBA

Leia's mission was a success. She cunningly convinced the Empire that she was recruiting new planets for the rebel cause in a distant corner of the galaxy. Soon, the Empire was scouring those planets for Alliance sympathizers, and ignoring the rest of the galaxy entirely. This was Leia's plan—with the Empire chasing *her*, they were ignoring the *real* action. Quietly, the Rebel Alliance began to amass a huge fleet of ships. Now they'd be able to meet the Empire in battle—and stand a chance of winning.

As soon as Princess Leia had completed her

Jabba the Hutt

Jabba was a crime lord who specialized in smuggling, piracy, and slavery. He was a ruthless kingpin, controlling a vast empire of crime from his headquarters on the Outer Rim planet of Tatooine. Not only was he a criminal, he was also willing to work with the evil Galactic Empire, supplying them with materials in exchange for the Empire looking the other way and ignoring his crimes.

assignment for the Rebel Alliance, she began planning a more personal mission. She was determined to rescue Han Solo from the clutches of the revolting Jabba the Hutt. Vader had frozen Han in carbonite before he turned him over to Jabba. And Jabba, instead of thawing Han out, had kept Han as a frozen trophy in his lair.

Jabba's palace of crime was on the Outer Rim planet of Tatooine—coincidentally the same planet where Leia's friend Luke Skywalker grew up. Together, Leia and Luke hatched a plan to save Han from Jabba.

The first step of the plan was for Lando Calrissian to gain access to Jabba's palace by posing as one of Jabba's guards. In a helmet that covered most of his face, Lando was unrecognizable. Nobody inside the palace gave him a second look. Then Leia arrived. Of course, she wasn't dressed as the famous Princess Leia. She was in disguise as a bounty hunter named Boushh, complete with a voice manipulator. She brought Chewbacca with her, and pretended that she had taken the huge Wookiee captive and was holding him for ransom. Chewbacca played along, and the two friends were brought before Jabba in his throne room.

But as soon as Leia had snuck away to unfreeze Han, Jabba discovered her ruse and took both her and Chewbacca prisoner. The rescue plan was going badly—now their only hope was Luke.

When Luke finally appeared at Jabba's palace, his voice was calm and low and he carried himself with a new confidence. His training with Yoda in the swamps of Dagobah had changed the young Jedi. But despite Luke's new powers, things seemed to go from bad to worse. Luke was captured and handed over to a terrifying monster in Jabba's dungeon.

Leia was in no position to help. On Jabba's orders, she had to sit with him as if she were one of his dancing girls, but she was actually a highly guarded prisoner.

Of course, all was not as it seemed. Using his Jedi training, Luke quickly defeated the monster. Furious, Jabba declared he would execute the Jedi and his friends.

The execution was to be a gory one. Jabba planned to feed the traitors to his favorite sand monster, the spear-toothed Sarlacc. As if it were a carnival, the palace guards and entertainers joined Jabba on a barge that hovered across the desert dunes. Leia was there, too, in chains.

Han and Luke, sentenced to death, were ferried on a separate ship. Leia could hardly watch as the guards prepared to force her friends into the gaping mouth of the Sarlacc, yet she trusted that Luke was resourceful. She prepared herself for a fight. When Luke made his move, Leia did, too. They both threw themselves into battle with Jabba's criminal underlings. Leia strangled Jabba with the very chains he'd used to bind her,

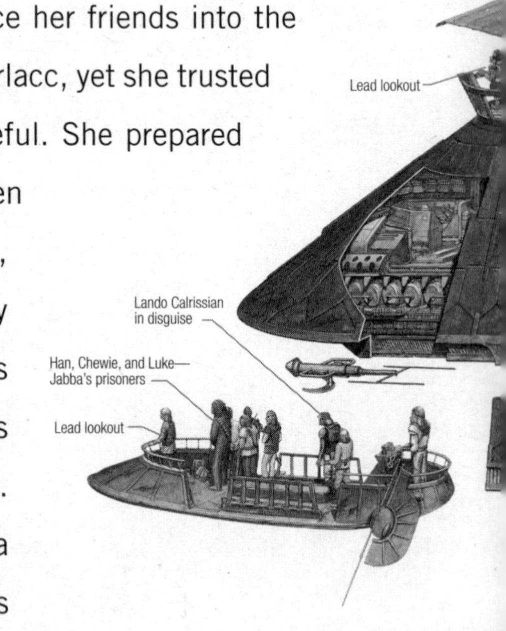

and she and her friends escaped Jabba's floating crime ship.

Behind them, the ship burned and reeled, finally exploding.

THE SAIL BARGE THAT JABBA RODE ON TO WITNESS THE LONG, SLOW EXECUTION OF HIS PRISONERS BY DIGESTION IN THE SARLACC PIT

CHAPTER NINE

THE ALLIANCE STRIKES BACK

With Han rescued, there was no time to spare. Leia said farewell to Luke Skywalker, who was going to visit his Jedi Master, Yoda, on Dagobah. Then she rounded up Han, Lando, and Chewbacca and the four friends hurried away from Tatooine to rejoin the Rebel Alliance.

Although Leia knew that the Alliance had collected a huge battle fleet, seeing it in person for the first time must have meant a lot to her. After all, this was proof that her hard work on the diversionary mission had been successful; the rebel fleet stretched as far as the eye could see through space . . . And they'd acquired the ships right under the Empire's nose, thanks to Leia.

In the war room in the heart of the Alliance's Headquarters Frigate, Leia watched as Mon Mothma laid out the situation. Mon Mothma was the leader of the Rebel Alliance, and one of the few people whom Leia

followed and obeyed without question; something about the leader made Leia restrain her typical headstrong and stubborn ways. Being a dedicated servant of the rebel cause, Leia had the deepest respect for Mon Mothma's brilliant strategies and her strong leadership.

The rebels' plan was simple. The Empire was building another Death Star, but it wasn't complete yet—and the Emperor himself was on board the vulnerable battle station! If the Alliance could disable the shield protecting this second Death Star, they would be able to destroy the battle station itself—and the Emperor along with it.

Princess Leia knew better than most how important it was that the Emperor be unseated—even destroyed. She'd met him once, as a young woman, when she'd first been elected senator of Alderaan. The Emperor hadn't said anything particularly threatening to Leia, but the encounter had troubled her deeply. Even as inexperienced as she had been, Leia could tell there was something deeply evil about the Emperor.

The rebel plan was solid. Lando would lead the attack on the Death Star while Leia and Han went with a small strike team to the forest moon of Endor, where the shield was generated. Everyone rushed into action, preparing for battle. Shortly before the strike team departed for Endor, Luke Skywalker appeared again. He'd finished his final visit with his Jedi Master, and he joined the strike team as well.

Leia, Han, Luke, and Chewie arrived with R2-D2 and C-3PO on Endor not long after. No one in the Alliance knew much about this sanctuary moon. Leia discovered quickly that its lush forests were mysterious and a little alarming.

Before they could reach the shield, Leia and her friends encountered Imperial biker scouts. In the midst of a battle, Leia found herself separated from the rest of her team. She was nearly captured, but at the last minute a tiny, furry warrior—a native of the forest moon—stepped in and helped her fight off the Imperial trooper.

THE DEATH STAR SHIELD, LOCATED ON THE FOREST MOON OF ENDOR.

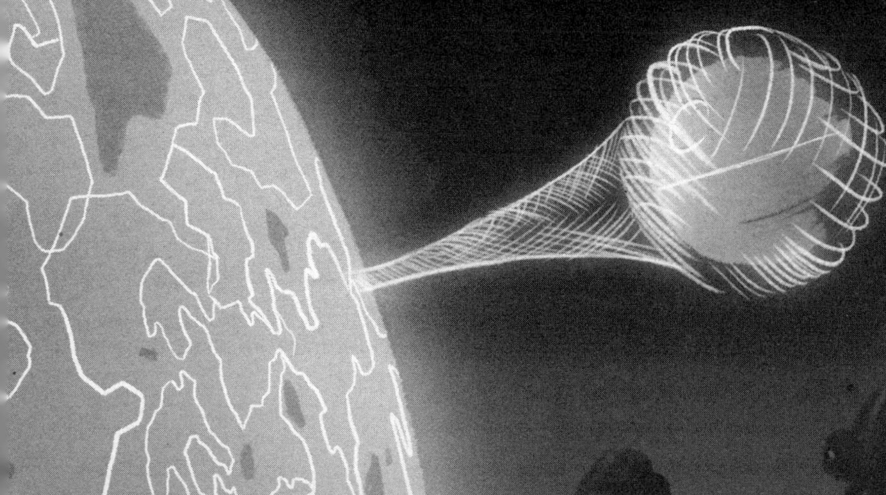

PROFILE

WICKET W. WARRICK

Wicket was an Ewok warrior and scout whose tribe lived in the dense forests of the moon of Endor. His unusual curiosity and bravery helped him approach and aid Princess Leia during her mission to destroy the Death Star's shield, and he attacked an Imperial scout on Leia's behalf.

Leia's new friend was an Ewok named Wicket. Wicket brought her to his village. Although she was worried about Han and Luke, Leia was confident that her friends could take care of themselves.

In their treetop village, the Ewoks treated Leia with kindness and respect—and intense curiosity. Although she didn't speak their language, Leia could tell from their expressions that they meant her no harm. When her small hosts gave her a hot meal, she ate it without worry.

Leia's efforts at communication would have been much smoother if she'd had C-3PO's language skills available to her. Luckily, the droid soon appeared, along with the rest of Leia's team. They had been captured by the Ewoks! Almost as troubling was the fact that the Ewoks believed C-3PO was some kind of god.

Luke used his Jedi powers to calm down the tiny forest warriors, and soon everyone was friends again.

With C-3PO's help, they were able to explain their mission to the Ewoks. That night, they all gathered by the fire for storytelling. The next day would be their only chance to destroy the shield generator that protected the Death Star.

But Leia didn't have much time to enjoy the gathering before a strange new development occurred. Luke pulled her aside and gave her the most surprising news of her life: Luke had learned the true identity of his father. It was none other than Darth Vader himself! This was disturbing enough, but it was followed by the revelation that Luke was Leia's twin brother. It was a difficult piece of news to absorb. Leia's birth father was a mass-murderer . . . but her brother was the last Jedi, a man who was dedicated to all that was light and good in the galaxy.

Luke's devotion to the Jedi path was admirable, but it was also taking him in a dangerous direction. He was determined to confront their father and do whatever he could to bring Anakin Skywalker back to the light.

All of Leia's stubbornness and diplomacy was no good in convincing him not to go.

Even level-headed, quick-witted Leia must have felt a great deal of confusion as she watched her brother leave to turn himself in to the Imperials so he could confront his father. But she had no time to dwell on it. She had a mission to accomplish—a shield to deactivate.

The new alliance with the Ewoks was good news for Leia's strike team. By themselves, they were outnumbered and outgunned. But with the Ewoks

THE BUNKER ON THE MOON OF ENDOR. IT HOUSED THE POWER ROOM FOR THE SHIELD THAT PROTECTED THE EMPIRE'S NEW DEATH STAR, AND IT HAD A SECRET BACK ENTRANCE.

Lando Calrissian

From his early days as a criminal and smuggler, Lando Calrissian moved on to a position of significant responsibility as the baron administrator of Cloud City on Bespin. But his most lasting—and famous—role in life was as a general for the Rebel Alliance. It was Calrissian himself who fired the killing strike at the second Death Star. In doing so, he effectively won the Galactic Civil War for the Alliance.

helping them and using innovative tactics, the rebels were able to get the upper hand in battle against the Imperials. Soon, the strike team had access to the Empire's bunker! There were setbacks and surprises along the way, but Leia and Han managed to destroy the shield generator.

Leia's victory on Endor happened just in time—shortly after the shield was disabled, Lando Calrissian, piloting the *Millennium Falcon*, led a team of fighters on a successful mission to destroy the new Death Star. The enormous explosion could be seen all the way across the system, and a great cheer went up from Leia's strike team when they saw the shower of fire and sparks that had once been the second Death Star.

With the destruction of the Empire's great battle station—and the deaths of Darth Vader and the Emperor himself—the tide finally turned for the Rebel Alliance. The Empire was no more, and the rebels were stronger than ever.

The era of the New Republic could begin.

CHAPTER TEN

GENERAL LEIA

The first two decades of Princess Leia's life are well documented. Her activities during the Galactic Civil War, especially the role she played in the destruction of the Empire, have been preserved in many histories of the galaxy. Even tales from her beginnings as a senator and spy are easy to find in old Alliance files.

But it is for the years following the civil war that there is less data available about the princess of Alderaan. She is now, of course, a general of the Resistance. But it seems that many of the records of Leia's life after her experience on Endor, such as her time as a young mother and as a New Republic leader, are missing. These records may have been lost when the First Order destroyed the system of Hosnian Prime. This lack of documentation has left anyone with a serious interest in Princess Leia Organa with no option but to speculate about many aspects of her life.

General Organa is known to be a very private person. Despite numerous requests, she has not agreed to fill in any gaps left by the official record—and she gave but a few brief accounts to an archival droid. Out of respect for her privacy, this biography does not guess what adventures might be missing from the official New Republic records. We include only what is verified.

What is known is this:

Shortly after the battle of Endor—and the downfall of the Galactic Empire—Leia Organa married Han Solo. They had one child, a son they named Ben.

In this time, Princess Leia's dedication to the New Republic was clear. She was a senator and needed to stay at the government's headquarters on Hosnian Prime. She defended the people, her beliefs fueled by her time as a rebel—and by the ideals of her adoptive parents and her birth mother. While her husband pursued racing prizes across the galaxy, Senator Organa attended countless meetings. She was devoted to the political process even when the divided opinions of the

two parties impeded any progress. While her heart was with her husband and son, her time belonged to the New Republic.

Taking after his mother, Ben proved to be Force-sensitive. When the time seemed right, Leia and Han sent their child to train with her brother, Luke Skywalker, a Jedi.

Luke had been the last surviving Jedi in the galaxy for many years. After the battle of Endor, he hoped to reestablish the Jedi Order.

But Luke's dream of rekindling that flame was tragically dashed to pieces. Ben Solo was seduced by the dark side, and by the First Order—a military movement that opposed the New Republic and the Jedi.

Leia's son killed all the apprentices Luke had been training and left his uncle's Jedi Temple in flames. Like his grandfather, he took a new name after turning to the dark side—Kylo Ren.

Luke abandoned his quest to rebuild the Jedi Order and vanished. It had now been years since Skywalker was last seen. Although General Leia had mounted

THE REMAINS OF DARTH VADER'S HELMET, THOUGHT TO BE CURRENTLY IN POSSESSION OF KYLO REN.

PROFILE

Han Solo

His background as a smuggler and criminal made Han Solo an unexpected figure in the Rebel Alliance. But few individuals have made a bigger difference in the history of the Republic than this dashing space pirate. Perhaps best known as the husband of General Leia Organa, Solo served as a rebel spy and general in several crucial battles, before returning to private enterprise toward the end of his life.

many search parties to find her missing brother, there had been no sign of him.

Following his grandfather's path, Kylo Ren became an apprentice to a powerful leader. His master was the Supreme Leader of the First Order, a mysterious figure named Snoke. The Supreme Leader had a massive weapon called Starkiller Base at his command. Snoke led the First Order to challenge the New Republic. Only Leia, who left the Senate and founded a resistance movement against the First Order, directly opposed them. She served as the movement's commander: General Organa.

But a small resistance movement—even one with a brilliant mind like Leia's leading it—is no match for a weapon the size of the Starkiller. Before the First Order could be stopped, they deployed their weapon and destroyed the headquarters of the New Republic, along with the entire system where they were located.

It was a huge tragedy. One can only imagine the sorrow General Leia must have felt at seeing the New

Republic she worked so hard to create destroyed in a single blow. But a more personal loss followed soon: In a confrontation on Starkiller Base, Kylo Ren struck down his own father, Han Solo.

Witnesses at the resistance base have said that Leia staggered and nearly collapsed at the exact moment her husband died, although his death occurred light years away, and there was no way she could have known. Perhaps she felt Han's death through the Force.

Led by Leia's best X-wing pilot, Poe Dameron, Resistance forces soon succeeded in destroying the First Order's weapon. But it was a hollow victory. The government of the New Republic had been destroyed, and the galaxy was in chaos. With Starkiller Base gone and her husband dead, Leia redoubled the search for her brother, Luke. She sent a Force-sensitive scavenger named Rey to find him, using galactic maps provided by the droids R2-D2 and BB-8.

There can be no question that the galaxy is badly out of balance at the present moment. With the New

Republic in tatters and the First Order rebuilding, there has never been a more vulnerable moment in our history. Although it is far from certain how the Republic might be rebuilt, General Organa seems convinced that the Jedi—and her brother, Luke—will be a key element in its salvation. History suggests that General Organa herself will play an instrumental role.

After all, Leia Organa is many things—princess, mother, spy, general—and above all else, she is a fighter.

Fast Facts

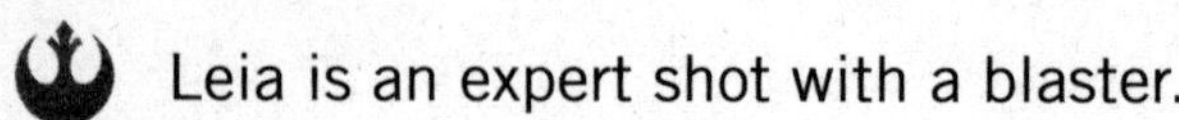

- Leia is an expert shot with a blaster.
- She's Darth Vader's daughter and shares the Skywalker Force-sensitivity.
- She's the only known surviving member of the royal family of Alderaan.
- She single-handedly strangled the notorious Jabba the Hutt to death.
- She once called Han Solo a nerf herder.
- She can resist mind probes and torture.
- She became a senator at just sixteen years old.
- She became a spy not long after, encouraged by her adoptive father.
- Princess Leia's party nominated her to run for the position of First Senator of the New Republic.
- She founded the Resistance herself and continues to lead it to this day.

Glossary

alliance: A group of people who have agreed to work together for a cause.

apprentice: A person who studies and practices a skill with someone who has significant experience.

biological: Related to life and living things; a biological parent is a natural parent, related by blood.

diplomatic: Showing the ability to handle matters carefully and politely, especially when dealing with governments.

droid: A mechanical being, like a robot, that is programmed with artificial intelligence.

empire: A government that often has many territories under the rule of one leader, who is typically called an emperor.

Force: An energy field that surrounds, binds, and connects all living things.

galactic: Related to a galaxy.

galaxy: One of the many groups of stars that make up the universe.

imperial: An adjective for something related to an empire or emperor.

Jedi: A Force-sensitive individual who studies and utilizes the mystical energy of the Force.

rebel: Someone who does not follow all the rules or who opposes the accepted way of doing things.

republic: A government where citizens elect officials.

resistance: The act of resisting or opposing, or a group of people working together against something.